# HOW TO LIVE WITH AN ENGINEER

*Camille Minichino, Ph.D.*

ISBN-13: 978-1490554402

ISBN-10: 1490554408

Cover Design and Layout: Richard P. Rufer

First edition

First printing: June 2013

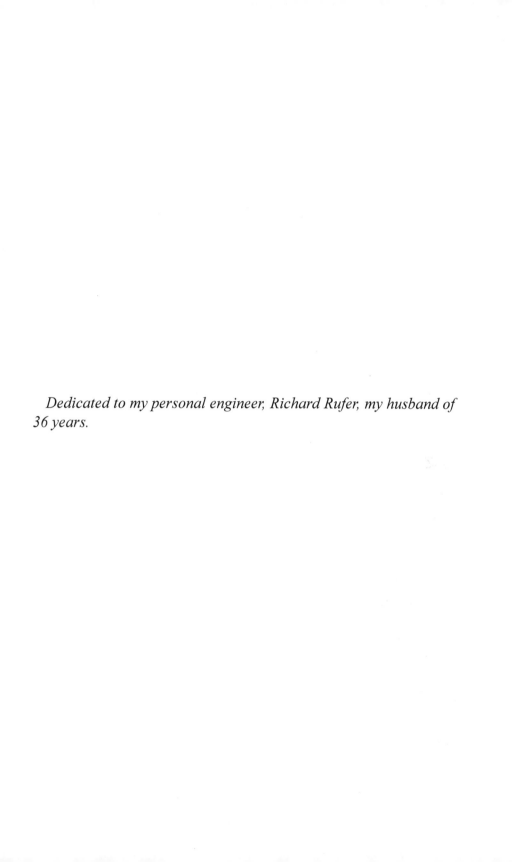

*Dedicated to my personal engineer, Richard Rufer, my husband of 36 years.*

# TABLE OF CONTENTS

# Preface

Fall, 1987. Open House was one week away at the national laboratory where I worked. Tour guides were prepped; unique project equipment was polished and ready for show and tell; balloons and cupcakes were on order. The families and friends of 8000 employees would descend on the 1-mile-square property and see what Dad or Mom did all day. It was an early "Take Your Family To Work" experience.

"We need something fun for the wives—uh, spouses," my boss said, correcting his sexist leanings. "The ones who aren't into tech stuff."

"Like a cooking show?" one guy suggested.

"Song and dance?" another techie offered.

"Relay races?" from another.

Nothing grabbed us.

"I could talk about how to live with an engineer," I said.

Cheers rose from the crowd.

That was the beginning. The original 1-hour talk, which seemed to resonate with the attendees (admittedly, mostly women), has taken many forms over the last three decades, including a day-long class in the logic of communication, special workshops for the laboratory's editorial, clerical, and budget staffs, and an audio tape that I sold at crafts fairs.

This book is the result of studying and teaching technical subjects, working with scientific and technical professionals, topped off with more than three decades of marriage to one special techie. "How to Live with an Engineer" provides insight and strategies for dealing with the techies we care about.

This e-book is the latest incarnation.

I hope you enjoy the book and also find something to think about.

.

# Introduction

Is there an engineer in your life? A techie who sometimes speaks a language you don't understand? I'm not talking about jargon, like bytes and routers and malware. I'm talking about how they don't seem to understand the plain English the rest of us use, how they give us strange looks in the middle of a conversation, how they ask questions like "Why are you driving in this lane?"

As the number of academic and professional degrees awarded in all fields of engineering continues to grow, it's hard to escape the techies that surround us, both at home and at the office.

We wouldn't want to live without them, those special, lovable, smart, helpful people. We laugh at engineer jokes:

*The optimist says the glass is half full; the pessimist says it's half empty. What does the engineer say? Answer: why is there twice as much glass as there needs to be?*

Funny, but not when it's your engineer and he or she appears to be hassling you over the size of glass you chose or the route you're taking to the mall. When it comes to social and personal interactions, the engineer's skills and training often work against him. "How to Live with an Engineer" is a blueprint for understanding the slightly peculiar traits of the species. The goal is to use the peculiarities to our advantage, to improve communication and common decision-making at all levels—from which paper plates are most effective, to how to save the planet.

The key is to understand how engineers were trained and how their training affects their everyday interactions.

Three characteristics stand out in communications with engineers: **they're troubleshooters, they love numbers,** and **they love to argue.** Understand these traits and never again be frustrated in an argument with a techie.

The payoff is improved communications and a happier, more productive environment at home or with the IT department at work.

# CHAPTER 1

# "HOW DO I LOOK?"— AN INVITATION TO TROUBLESHOOT

*A "no" uttered from the deepest conviction is better than a "yes" merely uttered to please, or worse, to avoid trouble.* -- Mahatma Gandhi (1869-1948)

The first techie trait that needs to be understood is that of troubleshooting. Most of us know how to do this when required—if an appliance doesn't work, we make sure it's plugged in, check the buttons and switches for loose connections, and maybe even check out removable parts. It's unlikely that we would do any of that if the appliance appeared to be working as expected. But the techie is always on the lookout for troubleshooting opportunities, even when there's no obvious problem.

Here's the scenario: You come into the room dressed for a party and ask, "How do I look?" Uh-oh. The engineer spouse immediately takes up the challenge and starts looking for problem areas. Even if your remark is not in the form of a question ("I guess this dress is okay for the party.") the engineer will begin a checklist to solve what he or she perceives as a problem. You shouldn't be surprised to hear something like this:

"First, the clanging noise from your bracelets might disturb the musicians. Second, you might find it hard to walk on Joe's new driveway in those heels. Third, with that sleeveless top, you're not going to be warm enough if we come home late."

Well, you did after all ask, "How do I look?"

The engineer logically assumes that if all you wanted to hear was, "You look great," or "Cool outfit," you would have said so.

In this chapter, we'll explore the first characteristic of engineers and other techies: they're constantly troubleshooting, looking for problems, and solving yours, whether you want them to or not.

It's not their fault! It's their training.

One of the main consequences of the training of engineers is a built-in troubleshooting mechanism that seems to operate at all times. He (only 14% of the total engineering workforce are female) looks for trouble. His job is to inspect a system—a circuit, a car, a bridge, a computer program—and ask himself where things have gone wrong, or where they might go wrong in the future.

If there's already a problem to solve, he begins by examining every possible piece of the item or project to determine where is the source of the trouble. If he's in the design stage of the project, he does the same thing, anticipating future problems and testing for potential failure under certain operating conditions.

A few years ago, when I'd come home from a long day at work and say, "I'm tired," my engineer husband's response was a helpful list of recommendations:

"Don't try to do so much tomorrow," he'd say, fiddling with his pocket protector. "Take a short nap before dinner; let's cancel part of our busy weekend schedule; and retract your offer to drive Mary to the doctor's."

When I remembered his training, I realized that I was setting him up to provide this list of solutions. He was solving the problem he thought I was giving him. Why else would I report, "I'm tired," unless I wanted ideas for becoming untired?

In my world, the question isn't really a question, but a way of unloading stress onto a sympathetic ear. I want to whine in a safe place. In his world, it's an invitation to troubleshoot. It's a problem crying out for a solution.

Happily, engineers are easy to deal with when they're given clear, specific instructions. Once you establish cues about what kind of response you want, the engineer can usually be counted on to follow directions exactly. With some coaching, my husband now understands that most of the time, if I tell him that I'm tired, or don't feel well, or feel pressured or tense, I just want him to rub my shoulders and say, "poor baby."

If I want advice, I ask explicitly: "Do you have any ideas about how I can make this week less hectic?" Or, "I'd appreciate help from you on two things that are crowding my schedule today." Expressions like this are his green light for welcome troubleshooting.

## Passive Troubleshooting

The troubleshooting attitude of engineers is at the root of why so many techies and engineers are not comfortable at parties or large social gatherings. Imagine hearing bits of conversation:

"My son is having trouble with geometry."

"My sister found out she has a tumor."

"I've been having difficulty climbing stairs lately."

"There's a good chance I'll lose my job this year."

Now imagine thinking that you have to solve all these problems. They're coming at you from all directions, and without much of a time interval between them. And you don't have your toolbox with you.

Engineers love to solve problems, but not in an environment that's out of their control, with people milling about, pursuing many lines of discussion at the same time. Staying home is a more relaxing option.

In another setting, with an opportunity for more organized discussion, when the engineer hears a father say, "My son is having trouble with geometry," he'll be only too happy to give advice.

"Maybe he needs a tutor," the engineer might say. "Have you talked to the geometry teacher? The pace of the class may be too fast, or maybe a college program isn't right for your son."

These last suggestions are not likely to be well-received by parents. It's not something they want to hear—that their son may not be the genius they think he is—no matter that they seem to be seeking advice.

The suggestion is even more unacceptable when they think they're simply sharing a concern with a sympathetic listener.

Logically, the suggestion that the child may not be up to a rigorous geometry class is a sound one. It certainly belongs on a list of possible reasons for the boy's trouble. This is all that matters to the techie. Often in these situations, the parents respond on an emotional level, interpreting the suggestion as an insult, which was not at all the techie's intent.

The party scenario presents an opportunity for what I call "passive troubleshooting" — attempts to solve problems that the speaker hasn't intended to present as a problem. This pattern is the basis for a great deal of misunderstood communication. Although their intent is to be helpful, when engineers troubleshoot, they're often seen as rude. (Later we'll see examples of "active troubleshooting"—where the engineer initiates an investigation.)

Here are other examples of passive troubleshooting, comments that trigger the engineer to solve a problem, whether or not you meant it to sound that way:

> **You:** I'll never get all this done by Friday.
> **What you want to hear:** Poor you, stuck with a demanding boss.
> **What your engineer says:** You've taken on too much. Ask your boss for an assistant. Maybe Helen can help you.
> **You:** I wish I didn't have to go that luncheon for Grace tomorrow.
> **What you want to hear:** Yes, too bad. What a drag.
> **What your engineer says:** You don't have to do anything you don't want to do. What do you owe Grace, anyway?

> **Exercise:** *Read through the examples. Think about times when your engineer has tried to help you by solving a problem you didn't know you were presenting. Write out the scenario as above. What did you really want to hear? What else could you have said in order to get the response you wanted? For example, how could you have expressed yourself if you simply wanted to hear, "Poor Mary?"*

## Active Troubleshooting

Another way that engineers interact is through "active troubleshooting." In this mode, the engineer makes a simple request for information, but is misunderstood as being flip, or critical, or sending an unpleasant message, or having a hidden meaning to his or her query.

Suppose you're in charge of the laundry, and your mate says, "The laundry hasn't been done yet. Is something wrong with the new washing machine?"

When you hear this, consciously or otherwise you might think about what would be in your mind if you were to ask such a question of someone. Coming from you, that kind of remark might be your way of giving a mild reprimand or criticism. It might even be your intent to do a little condescending nagging.

But coming from the troubleshooting techie it's almost always a genuine query and an offer of assistance. It's caring in a very practical way. You may be in charge of the laundry, but the engineer, at least in his mind, is in charge of the equipment. Since it's his job to keep the machinery working, he really does want to know if there's a problem with an appliance you depend on.

If there is a problem, he looks forward to fixing it. More than once I've gotten my engineer husband out of a slump or distracted him from a worrisome issue, by saying, "I think something's wrong with the toaster (or the DVD player or the flashlight)."

"Oh," he'll ask, suddenly interested in life again, "did it fail in operation?"

Studying this behavior provides us with an opportunity to learn more about the language of engineers and to avoid misunderstandings. It's a good example of how knowing the language habits, likes and dislikes of the other person leads to positive, useful discussions, just as it would with anyone who speaks a different language from us.

On the other hand, if we interpret the active troubleshooting question negatively, we're likely to respond negatively. This will confuse the engineer, and what follows will often be a prolonged, unnecessary conflict. In summary, the best approach always is to take the statements or questions literally, at their face value.

Here are some examples of active troubleshooting:

**Engineer's question:** When was the last time you used your sewing machine?
**You (interpreting negatively):** Are you calling me lazy? I've had a lot to do, keeping up with my job and this house. I don't have time to sew. Why are you criticizing me?
**What the engineer meant:** When was the last time you used your sewing machine?

**Explanation:** The engineer is concerned about efficiency—if the sewing machine is being used less often than the card table, then the two items should be arranged to make the card table more accessible.

**Engineer's question:** How many blouses do you need?
**You (interpreting negatively):** Are you calling me a spendthrift, with too many clothes? Are you saying I have much closet space? You have the whole garage for your stuff.
**What the engineer meant:** How many blouses do you need?

**Explanation:** The engineer is curious. How many blouses do you need? If you have fewer than you need, he'll buy one for your birthday; if you have more than you need, he'll help you sort through them and prepare a bag for a charity donation.

Here are similar questions that are representative of an engineer's active troubleshooting:

*Did you eat the last of the cookies?* (Data gathering, so he'll know whether to put two boxes of cookies on the list next time.)

*Are you ready to leave?* (More data gathering; does he have time to screw in a light bulb?)

*What's the point of this?* (Valentine's Day, for example.*)

* Remember that engineers often don't know social cues and rules.

They may not understand the conventions of holidays and present-giving in general.

**Exercise:** *Read through the examples. Think about times when a techie has tried to help you by asking a question that you misinterpreted as nagging or insulting.*

## Exact Answers

Try this for an appropriate response to the engineer in the laundry example above:

**Engineer:** You haven't done the laundry yet. Is something wrong with the new washing machine?
*You:* I'm only at about 75% on the laundry this week, due to an increased load from your mother's visit. I can be at 100% by the end of the week, if you take over the vacuuming.

Not only is communication improved, but you've had some fun with numbers (next chapter) and delegated a chore. Life is easier.

Clearly, the week's laundry is not an earth-shattering issue to be spending much time on. But the principle is the same no matter what the issue, and once the "exact answer" technique is learned, it can be used when the issue is earth-shattering.

This is no different from the trick you learn in mastering any new language: Make sure you've had a great deal of practice in communication before you're faced with a crisis. Suppose you were preparing for a trip to Europe. In the beginning, you'd learn relatively simple, often impractical phrases like "show me the train station," and "give me the book." Train stations in any country are really hard to miss, and you can ask for the book with a simple hand gesture. What you hope is that by the time you need to say something significant, with nuances and idiomatic expressions—"please don't shoot me"—you'll be fluent in the language.

Here are more examples of appropriate responses, using exact details, made up or not. Note how much simpler and more pleasant the conversation is.

**Question from engineer:** When was the last time you used your sewing machine?
**You:** I used it to make Jane's Halloween costume, and I'll use it again in about a week, when I start on Christmas crafts.
**Engineer's happy response:** Oh, then we'd better leave it where it is.

**Question from engineer:** How many blouses do you need?
**You:** I need three kinds of blouses: short-sleeved casual, long-sleeved casual, and dressy, in at least two colors each. Also, I need enough to be able to get through at least a whole week's events without doing a load of wash.
**Engineer's happy response:** Oh. Thanks for the data.

**Question from engineer:** What's the point of Valentine's Day?
**You:** It's a way of celebrating someone special. But since it's so commercialized, and since we give each other so much all through the year, I don't think we need to exchange presents on February 14. But maybe we could go out to dinner on another night when it will be less crowded.
**Engineer's happy response:** Great idea.

## I'm Here To Help

A few years ago, Donna, one of my students, presented this anecdote in class to illustrate how "cold" her techie husband Victor could be. See if you agree with me, that this was really an illustration of how caring Victor was.

A friend of theirs had died, and Donna and Victor were at a reception following the funeral. The widow, also a friend of theirs, said, "I don't know how I'm going to manage without Paul. I don't know how to take care of finances, or the car, and I don't know anything about running the business."

Victor responded, "Well, it looks like you'll either have to take a class, or find someone to take care of things. Maybe your niece and nephew can help. There are several good books out there, too. If you like, I'll give you the name of our financial advisor. He's very good with people who are beginners in dealing with money matters."

Donna reported being annoyed and embarrassed at this, apologizing to her friend, and later criticizing Victor for being insensitive. According to Donna, Victor should have realized that their friend wanted sympathy, not advice.

Consider the incident a different way. The room is filled with people offering Donna sympathy as they head out the door, leaving the widow to her own devices. Only Victor offers real help. He immediately zeroes in on Donna's problem and wants to share his resources. He's anxious to help solve the problem he thinks he was given. Which person in the room is the most sensitive?

A good role for Donna here is to compliment Victor on his helpfulness, while suggesting that he might have waited for a less stressful time for the widow.

**Exercise:** *What do you think of Victor's response? What do you think about Donna's interpretation? Has your view changed since reading this chapter? Have you been in a similar situation?*

As a contrast to the logical, helpful behavior of Victor, consider what happened to me at my campus bookstore when I was a graduate student. I went to the window, and asked the clerk behind the counter for a book of stamps.

**Clerk:** I can't sell you any today. I have only one book left.
**Me:** I only want one book.
**Clerk:** If I sell you this book, I won't have any for the next person.
**Me:** But I'm the next person. Someone has to get the last book. Why not me?
**Clerk:** Because then I won't have any for the next person.

**Me:** So, the person after me is going to get the stamps?
**Clerk (frustrated):** No, I can't be left without stamps for the next person.

I turned away, also frustrated. If the clerk were at all trained in logic, he would have thought about a way to solve the problem. He could have sold me the book and told the next customer that he was out of stamps. Two simple transactions, instead of many difficult ones. If he wanted to serve as many customers as possible with the remaining stamps, he could have broken up the book and sold smaller units. Among many possible solutions, he chose one that defied logic and common sense and resulted in a lot of angry customers.

If this incident happened today, I'd probably ask to speak to the manager, and maybe sue for discrimination. Though it happened nearly 30 years ago, that lapse of logic, combined with the unhelpful attitude, remains firm in my memory.

## Happy Birthday

Engineers like to get it right, so gift-giving occasions are a source of a great deal of tension. To them, giving a gift is like helping out, and they want to know exactly what will be a help, that is, an acceptable, useful gift. Those of us who like surprises are not likely to understand this mentality at first, but for a logical, troubleshooting personality "surprise" is a bad word. Surprise equates to a glitch, a bump in the plan, often signally that something that should be working is not working.

For us, this characteristic is another one of those opportunities to use a "foreign" personality trait to our own advantage. The best thing we can do for an engineer is to specify the gift we want. With great success, I've learned to tell my techie friends and relatives exactly what I want and where to get it.

"I'd like the blue sweater that's on sale now at Bloomingdale's, in size large," I say.

At that point, my engineer husband sighs with relief, and I know I've made his life easier. For some people, this sounds cold and against the spirit of gifts. But engineers take delight in providing something that's needed, something that's sure to bring pleasure or solve a problem.

In one class, a student asked if I thought that this kind of person is just not thoughtful enough, not bothering to observe and figure out what will make a pleasing present. My way of judging is this: If I ask for the blue sweater in large and my engineer buys it for me, he's being thoughtful. If he hears my request and then buys me a red sweater in size small, or a pair of yellow shoes, or purple tights—that's when I'd call him thoughtless.

The way to judge the value of the gift is in the intent of the giver. When you think about it, it's hard to beat a giver who does his best to find out exactly what will be wanted and needed. It would be unwise for me to list here all the "surprise" presents I've received from non-engineers that have since found their way to garage sales and second-hand stores.

As for being observant, this is certainly a characteristic of engineers, but their observations are connected to data collecting, and must be made systematically, over a long period of time. Thus, given enough time, engineers will gather enough data to feel confident about gift-giving, but only if the person they're observing has a readily identifiable pattern. For instance, suppose you think your wardrobe has a pattern of being casual, rather than formal. This pattern may not be obvious if your wardrobe includes a wide spectrum of colors, fabrics, and styles, however, and the engineer will still need specifications.

In another class, a student brought up this difficulty she had with the issue of gifts.

"My friends know exactly what I want already," she said. "Why doesn't my husband know me that well?"

My suspicion is that this is another case where your friends are more like you, rather than liking you more. Even if you and all your friends don't like the same things, you probably go shopping together and therefore have a lot of informal information and data-collecting opportunities about what the other person likes.

## The Shortest Distance Between Two Points

Engineers know the most efficient way to do things and the best way to get from one place to another. They don't just know a way to go from Bar Harbor, Maine to Stockton, California; they know the best way—the way that has the least number of signal lights, the straightest and best paved roads, the fewest semi trucks.

Their goal is to optimize all the variables.

"Why are you in this lane?" my troubleshooting husband often asks when I'm driving.

I know he's asking because he genuinely doesn't understand why I wouldn't instead be in the lane that's the fastest, closest to my exit, and/or generally offering the least difficulty in driving.

Whereas I might be in a particular lane simply because I'm distracted and hadn't thought much about it, he'd be in that lane only if he'd read or heard on the news that the "real" best lane is closed for construction.

At times like this, I'm not above telling a fib. So I might say, "Joan said that the correct lane has four new potholes which I'm afraid will damage our car."

"Good for you," he'd say.

Or, if I'm feeling a little adventuresome, I'll test his ability to accept a "smell the roses" decision.

"This lane puts me closer to the median strip and I like to see the spring flowers in my side mirror."

"Oh," he'd say.

Trouble breaks out, however, when I don't respect his need to troubleshoot the situation and I take his remark as a hassle. In that case the conversation is likely confrontational.

**Engineer:** Why are you in this lane?

**Me:** Why are you always criticizing my driving?

**Engineer:** The other lane is better for merging in the next mile.

**Me:** Don't you think I know as well as you how to get there?

**Engineer:** That doesn't explain why you're in this lane.

**Me:** Aarrggghhh!

And so on, for an unpleasant trip.

## Xtreme Troubleshooting

Finally, here's a classic story, handed down for generations in engineering schools:

*A priest, a lawyer, and an engineer are condemned to die by the guillotine.*

*First the priest lies down face up, and waits for the blade to fall. But the blade sticks, and according to the law, if the blade sticks the prisoner goes free. So the priest gets up and thanks God and claims that Truth has spared him.*

*The lawyer is next. Like the priest, he lies down and looks up at the blade. Once again the blade sticks in midair. The lawyer is free. He stands up and proclaims that Justice has saved him.*

*Finally, the engineer lies down and looks up at the blade. Just as the executioner is about to make his third attempt to drop the blade, the engineer lets out a cry: "Wait, wait," he says, "I see the problem!"*

If that's not loyalty to troubleshooting, what is?

# CHAPTER 2

# UNWINDING WITH ARITHMETIC

*The most savage controversies are those about matters as to which there is no good evidence either way. Persecution is used in theology, not in arithmetic.* -- Bertrand Russell (1872-1970)

Engineers use numbers nearly as often as they use words to describe a situation. Many of them get the same thrill from numbers that others get from what they think is a particularly beautiful piece of poetry or prose.

Respect for numbers is an important element in the way engineers and techies communicate. If they suspect that we don't share that respect, they're less apt to pay attention to any argument we make. In our house, if I say I'll be ready in "five minutes," I'd better mean it.

Engineers treat projects both at work and at home the way we were all taught to do word problems in algebra classes: be very specific, go from one step to the other with care, and complete the problem by finding the solution.

Finishing a project is at least as important to the engineer as starting it, and every bit as important as the process itself. This is true even if there's no other reward, such as a grade, or approval from someone else who might see it.

My engineer husband still applies those rules, even to his hobbies and leisure time activities. He works on crossword puzzles with the same perseverance and tenacity he applied in algebra classes decades years ago. Even though his puzzles aren't going to be graded by a teacher, nor seen by anyone else, he's still committed to completing them. It's a common sight to see him meticulously enter the final letters into the puzzle slots, then crumple the paper and toss it in the waste basket.

For most of us, finishing a task is accompanied by some other activity or sharing: publishing a manuscript, winning a trophy, or receiving a grade. For the engineer, the sense of completion and a toss into the round file are good enough.

Even when it's impossible to quantify an answer, engineers find a way to be accurate. They do this by being literal whether or not the context requires it. They answer questions as if they were on the witness stand in a courtroom. My friend, Beth, a computer graphics expert, does this time after time.

**Me:** Are you going to talk to your mother this evening?
**Beth:** I do plan to call her number and talk to her if she's home.

For most of us, this careful wording wouldn't be necessary. We'd answer "yes," to the question; we'd assume that everyone knows the call would have to be placed, and there would be a chance that Mother might not be home. But Beth, ever the software engineer, is as precise in ordinary interactions as she is at her computer terminal.

If you tell an engineer, "You're always rushing me," he's likely to respond, "I didn't rush you two Tuesdays ago."

When he says this, he's not being a wise-guy. (Well, hardly ever.) He's being accurate.

The observations in this chapter are intended to increase our understanding of people who have an unusual appreciation of numbers and an extreme need for accuracy. It's up to us to use this insight to the best advantage in communications. We'll see how this is connected to other characteristics of the language of engineers, especially their literal interpretation of words and phrases. We'll also examine how these characteristics can be misunderstood as a sign of coldness or insensitivity.

## Hot Numbers

Last month, my husband and I set out together to take the car for a tune-up. As we approached the service station, my husband passed it up and continued around the block. On the second time around, I questioned why he was doing this.

He smiled sheepishly and pointed to the odometer.

"It's within a few tenths of 80,000 miles," he said. "What if the mechanic drives the car around for a while to check it out?"

I knew immediately what he meant. He couldn't let anyone rob him of the thrill of seeing this milestone readout.

It's a characteristic of engineers and techies that they derive great pleasure from numbers. They appreciate numbers in the same way that others appreciate the rhythms of a sonnet or the colors of a sunset. Number-loving people get excited when a meter shows all 4's, or when the digital clock reads 5:55:55. If it happens also to show 55 degrees on the outside thermometer, we might open a bottle of champagne.

You can be sure that my programmer friend Beth was among the number-buffs who were ready to welcome 12:12:12 on the morning and evening of 12/12/12.

For the most part, we're amused by people with this quirk. We're not upset when someone we know looks upon new computer software as a toy, and actually enjoys solving complicated equations, or even balancing her checkbook. We're not likely to feel personally rejected that our number-loving friend or spouse finds it relaxing to try random multiplication and cube roots on a new calculator.

We may wonder if makes sense to take time from a busy day just to track down a two-dollar discrepancy in a bank statement. What makes sense to the engineer is the view that numbers are important, and worth the time it takes to get them right. Moreover, for the engineer or techie, working with numbers is recreation, not drudgery as it is for so many people.

Usually, we take these amusements to be what they truly represent—playing with numbers as a harmless pastime. And we're likely to forgive engineers their compulsions about exactness to the last penny. But when the calculation is made in the context of a personal interaction, we often respond differently.

Let's say your engineer brings you flowers.

**Me:** Wow, thanks for the flowers.
**Him:** These cost as much as two oil changes.

It's much harder in this case to remember that he's merely unwinding with a little arithmetic. He's solving an interesting, if nonexistent, problem in long division. He wonders how many times $29.99 goes into $69.95, just as a history major might wonder what the United States would be like if the Revolutionary War had turned out differently.

We don't accuse the history major of wishing that the results were different; we know he's just curious. In the same way, the techie doesn't necessarily wish he'd used his money for an oil change or two instead of flowers for you; he's just curious.

The techie is not placing a value on the relationship, nor on the recipient of his gift, as it might appear. He's simply sharing the results of a fun calculation.

## Happy Anniversary

The closest I've ever come to having an emotional reaction to one of my husband's "fun calculations" was on our fifth wedding anniversary. We were reading menus in our favorite restaurant when our waitress, an older woman, noticed my corsage (which cost as much as it did to have the lawnmower sharpened).

**Waitress:** "Your anniversary?"
We both smiled and nodded.
**Me:** Yes. Our fifth.
**Waitress (sighing):** I never made it to five.
An awkward moment for me. But not for my husband.
**Him:** I've made it to five twice.

My first, but fortunately unspoken thoughts, ran something like this: *"Oh, and how many more times do you think you'll make it to a fifth anniversary, and with whom?"*

The evening was saved when I remembered in time that my husband was thinking about numbers, not about marriage and divorce. Not about me or his ex-wife. Just numbers.

## Bigger Than A Bread Box?

It's sometimes hard for engineers to obtain the numerical information that's so important to them. Our friend Gail reported to us that the house she'd just visited with their realtor had enormous rooms. My engineer husband had questions.

**Engineer:** "How big?"
**Gail:** Oh, they were really big. You couldn't ask for more space.
**Engineer:** What, maybe a thirty-by-forty-foot family room?
**Gail:** The family room wasn't small, by any means. We'd definitely be able to fit our sofa and a big-screen TV."

My poor engineer! We've probably all had similar experiences, where a description very meaningful to a friend or relative was unbearably vague to us. I remember trying in vain to get exact quantities from my mother for certain recipes.

**Me:** How much flour?
**Ma:** Not too much.
**Me:** How long should I cook it?
**Ma:** Don't undercook it. And don't burn it."
**Me:** So, how long?
**Ma:** Just long enough.

One more example: I facilitate discussions at three book clubs. My usual procedure for initiating discussion is to have each participant rate the book on a scale of 1 to 10. One member refuses to do this. Instead, she uses a scale of small, medium, and large. For her, she explains, calling a book a 5 is too specific. She'd rather say she liked it "medium."

*Exercise: Think about your answers to "numerical" or "how-to" questions. Which kind of answer are you likely to give, my mother's or an engineer's? How specific are you? Write your typical response in following situations. Add your own questions/answers at the end.*

*What do you like to read?* (As an example: Gail would say, "just about anything;" an engineer would say, "Biographies of scientists and inventors, sometimes a whodunit, and news and sports magazines.")

*How did you make this gravy?*

*What's the weather there today?*

*How many people were at the lecture?*

*Others:*

## Rounding Off

Diane has been married to Phil, a high school mathematics teacher, for ten years. Here's a typical dialogue, as reported by Diane.

**Phil:** How much did you pay for this lamp?
**Diane:** About $20.
**Phil:** What's about $20? Don't you know how much you paid for it?
**Diane:** About $20 means about $20. It means not $2 and not $100. What does it matter? We're not poor.

After a few more tries and increased aggravation for both parties, Phil searches for the receipt and finds out for himself.

**Phil:** $29.95 plus tax is not $20.

**Diane:** I didn't say $20. I said about $20.

**Phil:** If you wanted to round off, you should have said, about $32.

**Diane:** That's still between $2 and $100.

And so on.

Diane is annoyed by Phil's insistence on exactness in what she thinks is a small matter. She interprets his insistence on accuracy to the penny as his lack of confidence in her ability to shop, to choose a lamp, even t balance a checkbook which, as Phil has probably pointed out, doesn't have a column labeled, "about".

What Diane doesn't realize is that the lamp and its cost are also small matters to Phil. But what isn't a small matter to him is Diane's apparent disregard for numbers. He has difficulty understanding her sloppiness when she's dealing with mathematical concepts and processes, which he loves and respects.

For number-people like Phil, a mathematics teacher to boot, with a great regard for numbers, even "rounding off" follows very strict rules.

So, if Diane had said, "$30, to the nearest dollar," the conversation would have ended there. Even if she'd said "$20, to the nearest dollar," the conversation would have ended. Although that's incorrect in this case, Diane would have sounded correct, and Phil wouldn't have checked the receipt.

I tried to help Diane, a literature major in college, understand this by making an analogy with her own respect for words. When she says "about $20," and doesn't think it's worth the trouble to be more accurate, it's as if Phil used a word or phrase carelessly.

Diane was able to come up with her own example.

Phil once commented on a new red dress Diane brought home. "That's a pretty gaudy dress," he'd said.

Diane, who's not a showy woman, was indignant. "It's bright," she responded, "it's not gaudy."

"Well," Phil said, "bright, gaudy, close enough. What's the difference?"

For a person like Phil, nuances in words are as troublesome as numbers are to many English majors.

## Just a Minute

The same kind of miscommunication occurs between Diane and Phil when she tells him she'll be ready in "five minutes." He doubts it. From past experience, he knows better. It would be much better for Diane to take the time to make a more accurate estimate.

"In twenty-three minutes" may sound too long for Diane to admit to. But if she does admit it and sounds as if she has respect for numbers, Phil will be happier. He'll then think that Diane really has a grip on the problem, and isn't trying to mislead him. She can correct the estimate later and still be considered respectful of numbers, an important part of interaction for Phil.

(Should Phil, in return, be more respectful of words when communicating with Diane? Absolutely. But that's another book.)

*Exercise: Recall an occasion when you took part in a "rounding off" discussion. Which side were you on? How could you have handled the issue differently?*

## Overworked and Underpaid

The work environment is another place in which care with numbers is a big factor in good communication, especially with an engineer boss, or working with the IT department.

An engineer executive might ask her secretary how long she expects a certain task to take. The secretary will do better if she provides a numerical answer, even if approximate, instead of vague verbal expressions. Instead of saying that the project will take "forever," or "it depends," the secretary could say "about two hours, if I do nothing else, but closer to three hours if I also have to answer phones and do the photocopying that's now in my in-box."

The boss will then have a clear choice: either postpone all the other projects her secretary has or take a chance with the longer estimate. In any case the boss knows how to interact with this answer, saving a lot of time and energy.

Here are examples of more effective communication with a number people. The best strategy is to combine care with numbers (which doesn't preclude making them up!) and good supporting reasons.

**Complaint:** I can't finish this by myself
**Alternative:** To complete this task, I need 3 days of full-time assistance from a clerk who knows our filing system.
**Supporting material:** Write out a timeline; determine the availability of assistance.

**Complaint:** My office is too small and really dark.
**Alternative:** I'd like to have twice as much light on my desk, and at least 50% more counter space. I've worked out two ways of achieving this; one would cost $1250, the other $500.
**Supporting task:** Design two plans for the office—one ideal arrangement, one acceptable alternative. If possible, determine tangible benefits for each, in terms of productivity. For example, in your new plan trips to another work area might be eliminated.

*Exercise: Think ahead to an up-coming negotiation at work or at home, especially one that concerns a deadline.*

*What might be your complaint?*

*What would be a more "engineering" way to put it?*

*What can you do to support your position in a well thought-out way?*

## Today is the Second Tuesday of the Month

Another tendency of engineers is to make numerical or simply factual observations about themselves, the world at large, their own behavior or that of others. My husband and our techie friends often make comments like the following, out of the blue, for no apparent reason:

"This is the first time this month that I've been on this freeway going west."

"As of today, I've exercised every feature on our new microwave oven."

"I've now worn every shirt I got for my birthday."

"This is the longest time I've gone without a meal in a restaurant."

We need to remind ourselves of this "hobby" when a number-person asks, "How long are you going to let your hair grow before you have it cut?"

As we saw in Chapter 1, this approach to the world reflects the techie's need to troubleshoot, solve problems, and collect information, all related to his or her love of numbers. It has nothing to do with nagging or destructive criticism.

The engineer or techie is always curious about data. How many haircuts does the average person get in a year? How long is long enough? If the long-haired person hears this question and says, "I'm going to let it grow two more inches," the engineer is satisfied, and the conversation is over.

But if the person misunderstands the motive behind the question, the conversation might proceed as follows:

**Long-Hair:** Why don't you like my long hair?
**Techie:** I don't have any feelings about your hair. I just want to know how long you're going to let it grow.
**Long-Hair:** Do you think long hair means I'm a drug addict?
**Techie:** No. Are you a drug addict?
**Long-Hair:** See. I knew that's what you were thinking.

The techie will be confused, and the whole conversation will probably deteriorate into unnecessary conflict.

## Logic and Reason Get Bad Press

It would take too long for me to list the movies and television shows that glorify emotion over reason, the heart over the mind. Think about how often the reasonable, sensible guy (or girl), often a "city type" gets the shaft in favor of the sweet, poetic, "let's wing it" person.

*Exercise: Choose several characters from popular movies or television shows. Analyze the characters' behavior for tendencies to be logical or not logical. Use these questions for starters:*

*In a conflict between a character who's reasonable and one who's emotional, which character is presented as more sympathetic?*

*In the entertainment media, does an intelligent, reasonable character also have a well-rounded, normal social life?*

*Who gets the hot girl/guy?*

## Where Are You Going? Out.

Have you ever called a friend with a small child, one old enough to answer the telephone but not old enough to interpret communication shortcuts?

**You:** Hello, Josh, is your mom home?
**Josh:** Yes.

Silence. Josh has answered your question. He's not being difficult. He has given you the information you asked for. It's your turn again.

Josh's literalness stems from his limited experience with the nuances of words, and his lack of a context for common usage. Adults know that, "Is your mom home?" really means, "If your mom is home, please call her to the phone."

The child isn't prepared to interpret all of this. Children are generally more comfortable with literal language, language that doesn't go beyond what he actually hears.

Scholars who study the conventions of language use sample conversations such as the following, to illustrate lack of a common context:

**Mother,** to child, on a rainy day, as the child is about to leave the house: Where's your raincoat?
**Child:** In the closet.
**Mother:** Put it on right now!

The child's response is related to what's called interpretive difference. Although you might expect a mother and child to share the same background from which to interpret language, many other factors come into play.

The mother's use of right now indicates annoyance on her part, since she probably interprets the child's answer as flip. But the child gave a true, literal answer to the mother's question.

If parents are more observant about their children's literalness in other settings, they're more likely to understand this kind of response. Notice, for example, the delight children take in knock-knock jokes and puns, like the classic "Is your refrigerator running?" ("Then you'd better catch it!")

Or this joke told to me by my friend's five-year-old daughter:

**Child, holding up two fingers:** Why doesn't Daddy use these fingers when he plays the piano?"
**Me:** I don't know. Tell me.
**Child:** Because they're mine.

Here's another example of a child pursuing a level of logic that we might also associate with an engineer. Sister Helen Prejean, the author of *Dead Man Walking*, tells this story.

A friend who's a lawyer is explaining to his child why the people on death row had to be put to death. The friend told the child that because the condemned prisoners had killed someone, they had to be executed by state officials.

The child then asked, "Then who kills the officials?"

Adults constantly deal with situations where the same word or phrase or even the same behavior has many different possibilities of interpretation, depending on the context.

**Husband:** Do you know where today's paper is?
**Wife:** I'll get it for you.

The wife and husband share the common context that's lacking in the child, and they bring that context into their dialogue. In this example, the woman has interpreted her husband's question about where the paper is as a request for her to take it to him. She's probably correct.

*Exercise 1: Which of these questions do you interpret as having a built-in request for action or some other, further meaning? Which ones are probably exactly what they seem to be on a literal level? Add some of your own.*

*Do you have a watch?*

*Are you tired?*

*Are you busy?*

*Where are my socks?*

*How are you?*

*Exercise 2: Recall a time when you might have interpreted an answer to your question as flip, when it was merely literal. Would a rephrasing help in any way?*

Literalness is a common characteristic of the communication style of engineers. They often respond as children do, for much the same reason, that is, lack of context. In the case of the child, he hasn't lived long enough to acquire context. In the case of the techie, for the sake of accuracy and correctness, his or her training has stripped away the habits of colloquial interpretation that adults normally build up.

Engineers and techies, therefore, often take the same approach as a child in the telephone situation above. Unless we understand this, we might be annoyed and consider this behavior uncooperative or contrary to a desire for good communication.

It's safe to assume in the light of this, that engineers make poor administrators. Here's a conversation that has occurred repeatedly between my friend Gloria and her partner, George:

**Gloria:** Doris just called me and said she called here earlier. Why didn't you tell me when I asked?
**George:** You asked if there were any messages. Doris said there was no message. She said she'd call you back later.
**Gloria:** But I just wanted to know if anyone called, whether or not there was a specific message.
**George:** Doris said she'd call you back. That was a message to me, not to you.

It takes a higher order of understanding to grasp what every good secretary knows. When someone asks, are there any messages, the question includes all categories, including did the phone ring this evening, was there any call from someone asking for me, or did anyone say he or she would call me back?

What finally solved her problem, Gloria tells me, was for her to ask the question: "Did anyone call for me, with or without a message for me?" Now, unless someone specifically commands George not to tell Gloria about the call, Gloria gets all her messages.

(Gloria could also have simply gone for separate phones.)

# Meeting the Media

One of the most excruciating sights is that of a scientist or engineer in the hands of "the media." Since nothing can keep the press from asking probing questions these days, in many major high-tech industries and laboratories "media training" has become a necessity.

As a participant in one of these workshops, I watched otherwise intelligent scientists, myself included, struggle to not answer questions exactly.

"How much radiation leaked from the chemistry building this morning?" the instructor would ask, playing the role of a newspaper person.

What we all wanted to say immediately was "3.6 millicuries."

It took an all-day workshop before we learned to not answer. We learned to say instead, "This laboratory is doing everything possible to contain the effluent and to keep the environment safe for all our neighbors."

Even in less critical situations such as interviews with celebrities, you'll notice the same evasiveness. The star will usually try to get her message out, no matter what the question.

**Interviewer:** I heard there was some tension on the set of your latest movie.
**Celebrity:** We all had such a great time working on John's script; he's such a really, really, great writer.
**Interviewer:** Isn't it true that Paula wanted so many changes that John almost fired her?

**Celebrity:** The best part of the whole thing, you know, was the whole cast, like, working together, with John, and everybody. We had a ball.

*Exercise 1: Analyze a typical interview or a political debate for answers that actually are evasions of the questions.*

*Exercise 2: Think about how often you fail to answer a question directly. How often do you give your own message instead of answering a question? What are some questions that might tempt you to avoid a direct answer?*

# CHAPTER 3

# ARGUING, NOT FIGHTING

*I always cheer up immensely if an attack is particularly wounding because I think, well, if they attack one personally, it means they have not a single political argument left.* -- Margaret Thatcher (1925-2013)

Techies are uncomfortable in conflict situations (fighting), but they love to argue.

What's the difference between arguing and fighting?

The clearest distinction I've ever heard came from a fourth grader. I'd introduced the topic in an elementary school class on critical thinking. I'd set up the program in an attempt to help children deal more logically with their needs and interactions. I asked the children to tell me what they thought the difference was between arguing and fighting. A fourth-grade boy raised his hand.

"When you argue," he said, "it's about **one thing.** When you fight, it's about **everything.**"

I've often wondered how life has worked out for that enlightened little kid!

Pursuing one thing in a logical sequence of steps is the engineer's preferred method of communicating. It's his or her guarantee of correctness. Unlike stubborn people, who stick to their point no matter what the data shows, techies will usually yield to data and correct reasoning. In this way, they're easier to deal with than mules, for example.

## Do the Right Thing

I'd had my new computer only for a week or so when I needed to use it to print dozens of postcards to announce a holiday open house. I'd figured out a way to get what I wanted, or nearly so. In my mind I didn't have time to learn how to do it correctly.

This "wrong way" that I'd discovered was close enough. The lines of print would be slightly off center, and there would be almost no bottom margin. I didn't care, as long as the information was there. But my husband cared a lot.

"If I keep trying to figure out the right way to do this," I told him, "I'll waste more cards."

"It's better to waste two dozen cards to do it right," he said, "than to waste no cards doing it the wrong way."

My husband's response was from his deep need to do things correctly. Although he sounded like a preacher from an inspirational television ministry, he was quite sincere.

I think of my computer the way I think of my car. I want it to be reliable, run smoothly, and require a minimum amount of maintenance. I'm not interested in how things work under the hood, nor in knowing any more about it than it takes to drive it. Quite a different attitude from that of engineer.

Techies read manuals—car manuals, computer software manuals, manuals that come with the toaster oven. When they need to use a certain feature of a piece of software, for example, they don't go to the index hoping for a quick fix. They've already read the entire manual and understand how each feature fits into the context of the whole software program.

Challenges arise, however, when the engineer carries this need to be thorough and correct over to everyday life and to ordinary conversation. Pursuing thoroughness and correctness in ordinary conversation is called arguing. Techies enjoy arguing the way the rest of us enjoy a well-executed drama or concert. But their arguing is often mistaken for fighting.

This chapter and the following are about the rules of informal logic, used in arguing—not the logic of intimidating symbols, but the logic of language use. Just as we'd brush up on our French before a trip to Paris, it's a good idea to brush up on the rules of arguing before we engage in conversation with an engineer.

How can we tell if an argument is correct, or " sound?" In this book, as in most logic texts, the word "argument" refers to any attempt to persuade someone by means of words or pictures, combined with a claim of reasonableness. Using these guidelines, any of the following can be called arguments, but **none of them is sound:**

"It's raining. Let's go to the movies."

"Jane is always late for meeting; she doesn't care about her job."

"He's a nerd. How can you date him?"

"He's divorced, so he shouldn't be elected President."

In the following pages we'll examine arguments like this and show why they fail the test of correctness, that is, how they embody a **fallacy.**


## "So" By Any Other Name

It's important not to think of arguments not as sporting events or political races, that are won or lost, but as conversational units, used to express truths and reach logical conclusions.

In our depression-leads-to-new-outfit example, the premise is *I'm depressed,* the conclusion is *I bought a new outfit.* The *so* in the sentence tells us that the speaker thinks he or she is making a correct argument.

Other words that flag the logical person to expect a rational argument include:

*thus*

*it follows that*

*which shows that*

*which proves that*

*from which we conclude*

*since*

*because*

*therefore*

*If ... then*

When we hear these phrases, we expect a logical argument, and are therefore justified in examining the argument for soundness. When we hear words associated with emotion or beliefs, on the other hand, it's a cue that the speaker is asking us to accept the statements without analysis. We either agree or not; we'd be wasting time looking for logic.

If we want to make sense to an engineer person, we have two choices at this point:

1. recast the argument, or

2. don't use logic-type words, like those in the list above. Instead use words like the following, which flag the onset of an emotional appeal, rather than an argument:

*I like*

*I love to*

*I prefer*

*I feel*

*It's my opinion that*

*From my experience*

*I believe*

*I have faith in*

*I hope*

These words and phrases are regarded as non-logical. They're not illogical, by the way, they're just not logical and therefore do not require supporting evidence. The best response to such a non-argument is usually "How interesting," or simply, "Oh."

## Recasting the Argument

Let's go back to "I'm depressed, so I bought a new outfit." And let's say we want to establish a logical connection between being depressed and a wardrobe upgrade. Maybe in your family new outfits and shopping for clothes are known cures for depression, but that's not universally understood. This connection must be stately explicitly for the engineer to recognize it as a sound argument.

Here's one way to do it:

"My depression is related to a feeling of boredom and stagnation.

When I shop for new clothes and buy a new outfit, I feel more confident and I'm inspired to take action in seeking new friends and activities.

New friends and activities relieve my feeling of boredom and stagnation, which is the basis of my depression."

The shorthand way of saying this is *I'm depressed, so I bought a new outfit.*

If you think this is cumbersome, take heart. Once established, the shorthand version will eventually be enough for the engineer. Moreover, what's more cumbersome than two people trying to communicate while speaking a different language?

The techie who asks, "What does being depressed have to do with buying a new outfit?" isn't being unkind. He or she really wants to know what that premise has to do with that conclusion. In the expanded version above, we've given all the premises that connect the two statements. The techie is happy. And so, therefore, are we. (*Feel free to fill in the blanks to make that a sound argument!*)

## The Emotional Route

Going back to our second alternative, let's see what happens if we simply choose not to use logic-type words.

To avoid giving a false logic cue to your listener, use non-logic openers. In our depression example, an alternative to establishing premises would be to say:

"It felt really good to buy this outfit."

The most likely response of the logical person in this case would be

"Oh."

He hears the word felt and realizes there's nothing to be gained by pursuing the statement. He determines that he's not being asked to agree with anything or to participate in an exciting argument. He's simply being given information. *"Oh"*

*Exercise: Take the sentences that are formulated incorrectly as arguments, at the beginning of this chapter, and turn them into either: 1) valid arguments or 2) non-logic statements that don't require proof. The sentences are repeated here for convenience:*

*It's raining. Let's go to the movies.*

*Jane is always late for meeting; she doesn't care about her job.*

*He's a nerd. How can you date him?*

*He's divorced, so he shouldn't be elected President.*

As an example, the last one could be expressed (reasonably) as:

*I feel that a divorced man doesn't have the perseverance it takes to be President.*

It can also be expressed (fallaciously) as:

*He's divorced, which is sinful. He shouldn't be elected President.*

In summary for this section, what the engineer insists on is simply this: if you imply that you have proved a point by using argument-like words then your conclusions must be able to stand up to examination. If you'd rather not bother making a correct argument, use feeling-type words.

## I Really Should ...

Other words that imply that an argument is being made include *should* and *have to*, in certain contexts.

In the sentence: "We should (or 'have to') visit my Aunt Elsie," *should* sounds like the conclusion of an argument that has already been made. An engineer is likely to have a negative reaction to a *should* or *would* sentence like this and say, for example:

*"We don't ever* have to *visit anybody."*

His answer sounds quite cold, but all he's really saying is, *"I haven't heard the premises that would lead to the conclusion that we have to visit your Aunt Elsie."*

Another possibility is that in his confusion the techie might bring up a contradictory premise, and inadvertently hit upon a sensitive issue such as:

*"I thought you didn't like your Aunt Elsie. Weren't you upset when she forgot your birthday?"*

So, how do you communicate what you want? Remember that to an engineer, communicating how you are thinking—that is, the method you use to think with—is at least as important as what you're saying. Here's one possible rephrasing that's sound:

"Although she's not my favorite relative, my Aunt Elsie was very good to me as a child, and she's now old, lonely, and forgetful.

Visiting people who are at that stage is a kind thing to do.

Visiting people who have been good to us in the past sets a good example for our children.

Visiting older relatives is a recognized way of maintaining continuity with our own history.

We are people who want to do kind, good things, and keep a connection with our families.

SO,

Visiting my Aunt Elsie is appropriate for us to do. 'Should' is a shorthand for this."

In this case, I've set up a few reasons for visiting. We could add others that quantify what's "reasonable"—once a month, for two hours each time, for example. When all of these assumptions are laid out explicitly, the engineer finds it much easier to accept a conclusion. Once again, he's not being difficult or cold, but simply correct.

Although it may be hard to believe, it's also quite possible that the engineer is on a genuine quest to better understand how personal and family relationships work. The image of the nerd isolated from social and family ties is not entirely accurate, but it usually is true that he hasn't studied human relationships, neither through psychology, nor through literature or history, as liberal arts majors have.

This curiosity in finding out how people handle complex relationships is easily misunderstood, especially when it's expressed in objective terms, such as "Do you owe your aunt a visit?"

In the next section this point comes up again in the context of friendship.

In all of these cases, remember that one option we always have is to say that we're not trying to communicate our wishes logically, nor are we trying to be persuasive in the logical sense, we simply *feel* like visiting Aunt Elsie, or we *believe* in visiting elderly relatives. This alerts the engineer not to expect a reasoned argument, and he's much more disposed to hear the real message.

The value to us in being careful with engineers is that we have the opportunity to examine our true reasons for doing things. *Should* no longer has a hold on us.

*Exercise:* *Examine the common "should" sentences below. Write out several hypothetical unspoken premises for each case. Does the conclusion hold up when all the premises are spelled out? Add sentences of your own and examine them for logical validity.*

*I should lose weight.*

*You should have Louis cut your hair.*

*You shouldn't skip breakfast.*

*I should go to the wedding.*

*He should have remembered my birthday.*

*She shouldn't be running for Congress.*

## Occupational Hazards

Now and then it's good to remind ourselves that it's not only scientists and engineers who bring their work, and their thinking style, home with them. Here's an example of an editor friend of mine who let her training in grammar influence how she handled an interaction with a neighbor.

One morning Judith, an top-notch editor, told me that she'd found a note on the windshield of her car. A neighbor had written a message about a problem with the way Judith's car was parked in the common lot. Judith talked on and on, telling me about the spelling errors in her neighbor's note, the lack of punctuation, and the "terrible grammar" he'd used.

"What was his problem with how your car was parked?" I asked.

"I have no idea," she replied, "all I noticed were his poor writing skills."

Judith, was reacting to poor English usage in the same way that engineers react to fallacies in an argument. Fair or not, her neighbor would have been more successful in making his point if he'd been careful with the rules of grammar.

In the next chapter, we consider logic traps—3 of the most common fallacies, those that sound like chalk scarping on a blackboard to an engineer. Commit these fallacies and the engineer will miss your real message, just as my editor friend, Judith, missed the message from her neighbor.

# CHAPTER 4

# LOGIC TRAPS: THE 3 MOST COMMON FALLACIES

*"Nobody thinks clearly, no matter what they pretend. Thinking's a dizzy business, a matter of catching as many of those foggy glimpses as you can and fitting them together the best you can. That's why people hang on so tight to their opinions; because, compared to the haphazard way in which they're arrived at, even the goofiest opinion seems wonderfully clear, sane, and self-evident. And if you let it get away from you, then you've got to dive back into that foggy muddle to wangle yourself out another to take its place."* -- Dashiell Hammett (1894-1961)

Although it seems like a backwards, or negative, approach, focusing on fallacies is the best way to understand good reasoning. The commonly held thesis is that if you're not committing fallacies, your argument is sound.

Every logic text presents its own list of fallacies, varying in length from a few to more than thirty, many with overlapping characteristics. Logic texts also differ in the names they give the fallacies, some holding on to the original Latin name—such as, *non seguitor*—and others translating or interpreting the term, in this case, the fallacy of "irrelevant reason." But the texts agree on one thing: that the study of fallacies is an excellent way to understand the flow of everyday conversation.

In this chapter we'll discuss three of the fallacies that appear in most texts, ones that we're likely to hear or use ourselves every day: 1) irrelevant reason; 2) hasty generalization; and 3) the straw man.

## Fallacy 1. Irrelevant Reason

This is one case where the Latin name for a fallacy may be more familiar than the English name. This logic trap is commonly called a *non seguitor* ("it does not follow"). It's the technical name for the example in the previous chapter: *I'm depressed, so I bought a new outfit.*

Advertisers commit this fallacy when they present problems we all have and would like to solve, and then introduce their product as the solution, without justifying the connection or backing it up with data. Think of advertisers' common technique of juxtaposing objects or concepts, through words and images, to imply some logical connection between them. We've all seen the pairing of the advertised car and a beautiful or handsome partner; a particular brand of wine (or mustard or coffee) and a romantic evening by the fire; a cereal or candy bar and a burst of energy; a touted shampoo and healthy good looks.

In personal interactions we often commit the fallacy of irrelevant reason by pairing disconnected ideas or behaviors: *I've cooked dinner for your relatives all week, so we should eat out tonight.*

The engineer sees no logical connection here, unless there has been a previously agreed upon equation. Maybe five meals with in-laws equals one meal in a restaurant. (Notice the combination of an equation and numbers. Use it whenever possible—an engineer is helpless in the face of this plan.)

In certain situations we can use irrelevant reasons freely without worrying about the fallacy, such as when we address friends who know us and can fill in the blanks of the argument. Arguments such as, *I'm exhausted from work today. Let's go to a movie,* are not strictly fallacious if the listener knows the steps in between:

*I'm exhausted from work. (Premise)*

*When I'm exhausted from work, I need entertainment.*

*Movies are entertainment for me.*

*(Therefore) Let's go to a movie.*

The fallacious aspect shows up when we try the argument on someone for whom any of the suppositions don't hold up. For some people, exhaustion from work leads to a need for rest or down time, not entertainment, and therefore, the conclusion would not be appropriate. For others, movies simply do not constitute entertainment.

In almost every workshop I hold, at least one student, usually a woman, will say, "Why should I bother dealing with someone who doesn't understand all those steps that I have in mind when I say something? My friends know me better than my husband."

Remember, once again, that our friends may only "know us better" because they're more like us, not necessarily because they like us better or care more about us.

*Exercise: Write out arguments with the irrelevant reason fallacy, perhaps one that you've used yourself or heard lately. Take one example from home, one from work or recreation, and one from a news source.*

## Fallacy 2. Hasty Generalization

Any time we take the data from one event or incident and use it to draw a conclusion, or formulate a law, about every event or similar events, we're committing the fallacy of hasty generalization. We've all been victims of laws and practices that come about this way.

A common example is the universal outlawing of a substance or practice because someone abused it in the past or might abuse it in the future. Say, ten years ago a secretary was caught stealing yellow lined pads. We all know an administrator who'd post a memo prohibiting secretaries from entering the yellow pad section of the stock room.

Another form of hasty generalization is the use of always or never, or the equivalent.

**You to your techie spouse:** You spend all day Sunday watching football.
**Husband:** Not all day, only from ten to seven.

Busted. On a technicality.

In this case, as usual, better results are obtained when we preempt the numbers defense:

**You to your techie spouse:** You watch football almost exclusively from ten to seven. I would like about one third of that time for family activities.
**Husband:** Sure!

A side benefit of this clear expression: we take the opportunity to think clearly and objectively and determine the real reason for our displeasure about Sunday football. Do we want the television set for a program we like? Do we want more attention during football time? Maybe ten minutes each hour to chat? An hour for a family board game, one that's not on a mobile device?

The benefits of clear thinking extend beyond the academic.

*Exercise: Recall a recent use of hasty generalization. How might you have been more exact? What insight do you get by the more correct formulation?*

**The Intensity Factor.** Another technique for handling the real meaning behind "you always" or "you never" is what I call the intensity factor. I might simply explain that the sound of football (in this case) is so aggravating, that each one hour segment seems like three hours to me. In other words, there's an increase in intensity by a factor of three, and thus the exaggeration ("always") is not as inappropriate as it first sounds.

**Engineer:** I see.

Of course, an acceptable number of hours still must be established, but this expression brings us closer to the reality of sounding more accurate. And we know from experience that even the appearance of accuracy is important to engineers.

## Fallacy 3. The Straw Man

The third fallacy we hear nearly every day is the straw man fallacy—equating a general, irrefutable premise, with one of the speaker's own making.

Suppose the argument is about whether your spouse will work overtime or accompany you on a camping trip. Because of the state of affairs at her job, she chooses to work. You rephrase her decision.

**You:** So, your job is more important to you than I am.

Uh-oh. You've set up a straw man, attempting to link your overall ranking in your spouse's life (which should be irrefutably #1) with this particular choice, as if the two are logically connected.

I found this fallacy recently in a respected Op-Ed page when an editor was writing against a proposed cut in food stamps. The argument closed with, "The richest country in the world would strip its citizens of the ironclad right not to starve."

Never mind the *fallacy of unknowable statistics* (coming in the next book of this series!), the editor equated the right to life with a particular government program. Without taking a position for or against either budget cuts or food stamps, analyze the argument for its logical power: the arguer distorts the real problem (look into budget cuts and food stamps), and then argues against the distorted version (that citizens should not starve).

One more example: another editorial writer criticized women who use the title *Ms.*, so that like their male counterparts, their marital status won't be revealed by a form of address. *Isn't it a fact,* the writer argued, *that this particular woman is or isn't married? Don't we approve of facts?* Ouch! This fallacious argument would hurt the brain of anyone, techie or not. The writer set up a straw man that's not refutable—*facts are good*—and equated it with the need to use marriage-specific titles.

Here are a few other opening lines that signal a straw man fallacy:

"Don't I deserve a vacation?"

"Don't you care about your children's future?"

"Is your smile all it can be?"

"I guess my birthday means nothing to you."

And from the ever-present telemarketer:

"Are your utility bills too high? Call Gary's Aluminum Siding.

**Good response:** "I don't answer straw men questions!"

*Exercise 1: Write out arguments with straw man fallacy, perhaps one that you've used yourself or heard lately. Take one example from home, one from work or recreation, and one from a news source.*

*Exercise 2: At a rally against deregulation on environmental issues, a sign read, "Cast your vote for a nicer earth." How is this a straw man fallacy?*

## Life Is Not A Rally

An emotional, fallacious appeal is as likely to persuade some people as a well-reasoned argument. In some quarters, in fact, it's fashionable to talk about "living life" instead of "thinking about living it."

I call this the "life is a rally" view, where opinions and suggestions are yelled out, with loud music in the background and a host of balloons, bumper stickers, and T-shirts to match. Sounds like a good way to have fun, but not a good way to make decisions, to persuade or be persuaded.

My idea of the best environment for making decisions and forming opinions is closer to that of Socrates: The unexamined life is not worth living. Thanks to the engineers and techies in our lives, who help us remember.

## About the Author

Camille Minichino, a retired physicist turned writer, has taught logic and critical thinking at colleges on the both the east and west coasts. Visit her website, http://www.minichino.com, and blog http://www.minichino.com/wordpress

## Selected publications:

### *As Camille Minichino*

**Nonfiction**

Nuclear Waste Management Abstracts

How to Live with an Engineer

**Fiction**

The Hydrogen Murder

The Helium Murder

The Lithium Murder

The Beryllium Murder

The Boric Acid Murder

The Carbon Murder

The Nitrogen Murder

The Oxygen Murder


### *As Margaret Grace:*

Murder in Miniature

Mayhem in Miniature

Malice in Miniature

Mourning in Miniature

Monster in Miniature

Mix-up in Miniature

Madness in Miniature

### *As Ada Madison:*

The Square Root of Murder

The Probability of Murder

A Function of Murder

The Quotient of Murder

Made in the USA
Middletown, DE
24 July 2018